Indian-born DEBJANI CHATTERJEE and Anglo-Irish poet BRIAN D'ARCY are a highly regarded husband and wife team whose work is popular in anthologies for children. After many years teaching and lecturing, they are now full-time writers who have written and edited over 60 books. Debjani's books include *Animal Antics,* created during a writing residency at Sheffield Children's Hospital, the award-winning *The Elephant-Headed God and Other Hindu Tales* and most recently *Monkey King's Party.* Her many honours include an honorary doctorate and an MBE. Brian enjoys writing funny limericks, sober sonnets and tragic villanelles. His books include *Tha Shein Ukrosh: Indeed the Hunger,* poems about the Irish Famine, and jointly with Debjani, *Let's Celebrate! Festival Poems from Around the World.* They live in Sheffield.

SHIRIN ADL was born in the UK but was brought up in Iran. She studied Illustration at Loughborough University, going on to win the Hallmark M & S Talented Designer Award. She was Booktrust's official illustrator for Children's Book Week in 2010. She is the illustrator of *Ramadan Moon* with Na'ima B Robert, *Let's Celebrate! Festival Poems from Around the World* with Debjani Chatterjee and Brian D'Arcy, *Pea Boy: Stories from Iran* and *Shahnameh, the Persian Book of Kings,* both with Elizabeth Laird. She also wrote *I is for Iran,* with photographs by her husband, Kamyar Adl. Her latest picture book, which she both wrote and illustrated, is *The Book of Dreams.* She lives in Oxford with her husband and young son.

AUTHORS' NOTE

When we had the idea for this anthology we decided not to try to include poems for every game and sport –
that would have been impossible. And we don't claim that the poems in our book are about
the most important games and sports – everyone has their own favourites. But we hope that our selection
may tempt you to compile your own collection of poems about YOUR favourite games and sports.
Or maybe you could write your own poems about them? Most of all, we hope that,
when you look at our book, you have fun!

For Disha, Shreya & Aarav who make us proud – Munnu Pishi & Uncle Brian
For my ski buddies Shadi, Nader and Roshanak – SA

The publishers and editors would like to thank the following for permission to reprint their copyright material:
Muhammad Ali and Drew Bundini Brown for *Boxing Poem* (extract) copyright © 1964 Muhammad Ali and Drew Bundini Brown; Ann Atkinson for *Shot Put* copyright © 2001 Ann Atkinson, in *From Matlock to Mamelodi* (Derbyshire County Council); Ryan Banks for *Hockey* copyright © and *Baseball* copyright © Sports Series; Ann Bonner for *Netball* copyright © 1999 Ann Bonner, in *School Poems*, edited by Jennifer Curry (Scholastic); Grace Butcher for *Basketball* copyright © 2001 Grace Butcher, in *Girls Got Game* edited by Sue Macy (Henry Holt and Co); Debjani Chatterjee for *Chess Haiku* copyright © 2009 Debjani Chatterjee, in *Words Spit & Splinter* by Debjani Chatterjee (Redbeck Press); Mandy Coe for *Olympic Diver in a Holiday Pool* copyright © 2013 Mandy Coe; Denny Davis for *Swimming Lesson* copyright © 2011 Denny Davis, in www.dennydavis.net/poemfiles; Bashabi Fraser for *A Skipping Game* copyright © 2005 Bashabi Fraser, in *Masala: Poems from India, Bangladesh, Pakistan and Sri Lanka*, edited by Debjani Chatterjee (Macmillan Children's Books);Wes Magee for *The Skater Boys* copyright © 2013 Wes Magee, in *Here Come the Creatures* (Frances Lincoln); Asit Maitra for *The New Gavaskar* copyright © 2005 Asit Maitra, in *Masala: Poems from India, Bangladesh, Pakistan and Sri Lanka*, edited by Debjani Chatterjee (Macmillan Children's Books); *Right Royal* (extract) reprinted by kind permission of The Society of Authors as the literary representatives of the Estate of John Masefield; Kenn Nesbitt for *The World's Fastest Bicycle* copyright © 2001 Kenn Nesbitt, in *The Aliens Have Landed at Our School!* (Meadowbrook Press) and *My Puppy Punched Me in the Eye* copyright © 2009 Kenn Nesbitt, in *My Hippo Has the Hiccups* by Kenn Nesbitt (Sourcebooks Jabberwocky); Jack Norworth for *Take Me Out to the Ball Game* copyright © 1908 Jack Norworth, (York Music Company); Greg Pincus for *Tennis Doubles Trouble* copyright © 2008 Greg Pincus, in http://gottabook.blogspot.com/2008/04/tennis-doubles-trouble-tennis-poem.html; Philip S Porter for *On the Outside a Judoka...* translation copyright © Philip S Porter, placed on JudoInfo.com by George Weers; Charles Thomson for *Computer Game* copyright © 1999 Charles Thomson, in *Unzip Your Lips Again* chosen by Paul Cookson (Macmillan Children's Books); Grace Nichols for *When My Friend Anita Runs* copyright © 2011 Grace Nichols, in *Green Glass Beads* edited by Jacqueline Wilson (Macmillan); Grantland Rice for *Alumnus Football* (Extract) copyright © Nov. 2,1914 Grantland Rice, in Pittsburg Post-Gazette; Roger Stevens for *The Football Team* copyright © 2010 Roger Stevens, in *On My Way to School I Saw a Dinosaur* (A & C Black); Sasha Walker/Mills for *Surfing* copyright © Sasha Walker/Mills,placed on http://thebluegrassspecial.com in 2001 by David McGee; Rob Walton for *Scrabble* copyright © 2013 Rob Walton; and *4 X 100m* copyright © 2013 Rob Walton; Colin West for *Toboggan* copyright © 2001 Colin West, in *The Big Book of Nonsense* by Colin West (Hutchinson); David Whitehead for *Toboggan* copyright © 1998 David Whitehead, in *Secrets*, edited by Judith Nicholls (Ginn); River Wolton for *Pole Vault* copyright © 2013 River Wolton (commissioned by Derbyshire County Council as part of the region's Cultural Olympiad programme).

The editors and publishers apologise to any copyright holders they have been unable to trace, and would be pleased to hear from them.

JANETTA OTTER-BARRY BOOKS

Let's Play! Poems about Sports and Games copyright © Frances Lincoln Limited 2013
This selection copyright © Debjani Chatterjee and Brian D'Arcy 2013
Kite Flying copyright © Debjani Chatterjee 2013
Shaap-Ludo (*Snakes and Ladders*) translation copyright © Debjani Chatterjee 2013
My Pony copyright © Brian D'Arcy 2013
Let's Play Ping-Pong! copyright © Dr Debjani Chatterjee and Brian D'Arcy 2013

First published in Great Britain in 2013 and in the USA in 2014 by
Frances Lincoln Limited, 74-77 White Lion Street, London N1 9PF
www.franceslincoln.com

This edition first published in paperback in Great Britain and in the USA in 2014.

A CIP catalogue record for this book is available from the British Library.

ISBN 978-1-84780-584-3

Illustrated with watercolour, colour pencil and collage

Printed in China

1 3 5 7 9 8 6 4 2

LET'S PLAY!

POEMS ABOUT **SPORTS** AND **GAMES** FROM AROUND THE **WORLD**

EDITED BY

Debjani Chatterjee & Brian D'Arcy

ILLUSTRATED BY

Shirin Adl

F

FRANCES LINCOLN
CHILDREN'S BOOKS

Contents

PLAY THE GAME

Vitai Lampada (extract)

There's a breathless hush in the Close tonight –
Ten to make and the match to win –
A bumping pitch and a blinding light,
An hour to play and the last man in.
And it's not for the sake of the ribboned coat,
Or the selfish hope of a season's fame,
But his Captain's hand on his shoulder smote –
'Play up! play up! and play the game!'

Sir Henry Newbolt
UK

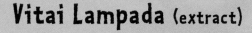

The New Gavaskar

I have pinned a poster
Of Sunil Gavaskar*
In my bedroom.
I keep all his scores.
I practise his stance
At the batting crease
Behind closed doors.
But they won't let me in
The school cricket team.

I play with my brothers, cousins –
We make up just seven.
On Sunday mornings
We gather our battered ball,
A bat, stumps, odd pad or two
And then march down
The sleepy Calcutta lane
To our pitch – a small
Half-grass half-mud field.

We play like shadows
In the mist. And shout 'Catch it',
'How's that'. Swap pad or
Bat. All of us chase the ball
When hit in case it is lost.
One day it hits my thumb.
I don't cry then or in Casualty.
Later I show my mates the old nail
Like a reserved ticket to fame.

I know my school misses me –
The new Gavaskar for the MCC*.

Asit Maitra
India & UK

*Sunil Gavaskar: an Indian cricket hero.

*MCC: Maitra Cricket Club

SWINGING

The Swing

How do you like to go up in a swing,
     Up in the air so blue?
Oh, I do think it the pleasantest thing
     Ever a child can do!

Up in the air and over the wall,
     Till I can see so wide,
River and trees and cattle and all
     Over the countryside –

Till I look down on the garden green,
     Down on the roof so brown –
Up in the air I go flying again,
     Up in the air and down!

Robert Louis Stevenson
UK

A Skipping Game

Skip one and skip two

Chicken korma with pilau.
Skip three and skip four

Mamma's pizza to your door.
Skip five and skip six

Chinese noodles with chopsticks.
Skip seven and skip eight

Fish 'n' chips on a paper plate.
Skip nine and skip ten

I'll eat out and you'll eat in!

Bashabi Fraser
India & UK

CIRCLE GAME

A-tisket A-tasket

A-tisket a-tasket
A green and yellow basket
I sent a letter to my love
And on the way I dropped it.

I dropped it, I dropped it
Yes, on the way I dropped it
A little girlie picked it up
And put it in her pocket.

Traditional circle game rhyme
USA

Tic Tac Toe

Tic tac toe, give me an x, give me an o
3 times around the world
Rock Paper Scissors shoot
Rock beats scissors
Paper beats rock
Scissors beats paper
I win, you lose
Now you get a big
fat bruise
and give them a touch
with your pinky

Traditional Clapping Rhyme
USA

I Wouldn't go to Missie

I wouldn't go to Missie
    Any more, more, more
There's a big fat police
    At the door, door, door

He will hold me by the collar
    And make me pay a dollar
And a dollar is a dollar
    So I wouldn't go to Missie
Any more, more, more

Traditional Clapping Rhyme
Caribbean

SCRABBLE

Scrabble

Scrabble, Scrabble

My letters spelt T R A B B L E.

Which is what I was in.

Rob Walton
UK

T R A B B B L E

Y U M L U N C H

S N A P C R O C

Chess Haiku

Chessmen from Bengal
played an imperial game:
their moves brought us here.

Debjani Chatterjee
India & UK

SNAKES AND LADDERS

Shaap-Ludo

There's a great many snakes
  before me writhe.
    But know no fear, ladders
      keep me alive.
    Some snake may swallow me
  out of the blue.
But know no fear, I'll come
  back good as new!
    The truth is we're all pals.
      They act as though
      they'll eat me up – and I
  too act scared. So
I'll just slide down a bit
  if an adder
    grabs me, then for sure I'll
      scale a ladder!
    Reaching the hundredth square,
  I'm home and clear.
Who needs jungles when we
  play with snakes here!

Susmita Bhattacharya
India. Translated from Bengali
by Debjani Chatterjee

Computer Game

WHAM! WHAM! Zappa zappa!
Zappa zappa zoom!
There's a manic computer game
up in my room.

As soon as I switch off
the lamp every night
enemy space ships
appear on the right.

ZOOP-ZOOP! ZOOP-ZOOP!
Beep-beep-beep.
The noises it makes
stop me going to sleep.

Now as the main
invasion fleet nears
I snug in my pillow
with plugs in my ears.

ZAPOW! ZAP! ZAP-ZAP!
ZAP! POW-POW!
As you may have guessed,
I'm wide awake now.

Zip-zip! Zeep-zeep!
Zip! BAM-BAM!
The rockets rush,
the lasers slam,

the deck guns splat,
the ray guns blast,
each invader explodes
as it rushes past.

Bip-bip, bip-bip,
zeep-zeep Zam!
Just one to go – look out!
BAM! BAM!

My ship is moving
in the deep.
Beep-beep, beep-beep,
beep beep beep.

The sky is black,
my ship is steady;
I open my eyes –
it's morning already!

Charles Thomson
UK

SWIMMING

Swimming Lesson

Swimming is an easy thing,
If you know how to do it.
You push the water wide apart,
And then you just go through it.

Denny Davis
USA

Olympic Diver in a Holiday Pool

Everyone stops, mid-shriek, mid-splash,
a striped red beach-ball pauses in its arc.
We squint to see him high against the sun
as he plunges – an arrow fired from the sky –
no splash, no waves. If you closed your eyes
you would not hear this dive,
only the soft blow of breath as he emerges
flicking water from his hair. Then the trickle
of water leaving him as he leaves it,
boosting himself up and out to pad across
warm tiles, nothing left but a trail
of drying footprints, the gaze of envious faces.

Mandy Coe
UK

SHOT PUT

Shot Put

(inspired by *Yasmin Spencer: Junior Women's Shot Put Champion*)

Three hours a day, six days a week for years
and years, priming the power in my muscles,
steeling the springs of my mind, for this
and now – the familiar weight
cupped in my hand, the cold curve
on the pulse in my neck.
Turn my back to the field, turn into my heart,
find balance, then all of my gathered strength
flows into the dance, hop and swoop, perfect turn
and the fire forges through me into the thrust,
all the hours and weeks and years of it, launching,
propelling four kilos of steel up, far and away.

Ann Atkinson
UK

Pole Vault

My ancestors were kin to bridges,
helped fen-dwellers jump ditches.
I can snap, prove deadly,
I have limits, test me.
Hurtle with me through the air
then plant me, I am tree
I turn momentum
into energy.
Leap, and for the second
that I point at sky
I'm astronomer, amazed
to see a girl who flies.

River Wolton
UK

CYCLING

The World's Fastest Bicycle

My bicycle's the fastest
that the world has ever seen;
it has supersonic engines
and a flame-retardant sheen.
My bicycle will travel
a gazillion miles an hour –
it has rockets on the handlebars
for supplemental power.
The pedals both are jet-propelled
to help you pedal faster,
and the shifter is equipped
with an electric turbo-blaster.
The fender has a parachute
in case you need to brake.
Yes, my bike is undeniably
the fastest one they make.
My bicycle's incredible!
I love the way it feels,
and I'll like it even more
when Dad removes the training wheels.

Kenn Nesbitt
USA

4 x 100m

My team prepares for the relay race
Pace up and down on the track
Baton in the first runner's hand
Number on her back

Gun cracks and away she sprints
First runner round first bend
Change over goes so smoothly
First runner's leg at an end

Back straight speeding for sprinter two
Gaps begin to appear
Our third runner caught by opponent's spike
When medals were getting near

I'm the final runner on the final leg
Fast down the final straight
Eyeballs out, racing for the line
Two hundredths of a second too late.

Rob Walton
UK

When My Friend Anita Runs

When my friend Anita runs
she runs straight into the headalong –
legs flashing over grass, daisies, mounds.

When my friend Anita runs
she sticks out her chest like an Olympic
champion – face all serious concentration.

And you'll never catch her looking around,
until she flies into the invisible tape
that says, she's won.

Then she turns to give me
this big grin and hug.

O to be able to run like Anita,
run like Anita,
Who runs like a cheetah.
If only, just for once, I could beat her.

Grace Nichols
Guyana & UK

TOBOGGANING

Toboggan

To begin to toboggan, first buy a toboggan,
But don't buy too big a toboggan.
(A too big a toboggan is not a toboggan
To buy to begin to toboggan.)

Colin West
UK

Toboggan

Take me where the snow lies deep
On some hillside high and steep.
Boldly sit astride my sleigh
One good push and I'm away.
Going speeding down the hill.
Getting faster – what a thrill!
At the bottom brush off snow.
Now to the top for another go.

David Whitehead
UK

30

ICE HOCKEY

Hockey

As I skate down the ice
With three seconds on the clock
The crowd goes wild, my team is in shock
As I get to the goal and shoot the puck
Zing it goes right in
What good luck.

Ryan Banks
USA

SKATEBOARDING

The Skater Boys

Last Saturday, walking the dog,
I passed a pub called 'The Three Lamps',
then stopped opposite the skatepark
where skater boys, on concrete ramps,
were performing daredevil stunts.
Hm. This wasn't collecting stamps!

The older ones, in t-shirts, jeans,
made high-speed runs down the steep hill,
did twists, turns, jumps, leaps and kickflips.
Fearless. A demo of sheer skill.
Then they'd stop dead at the ramp top,
casually catching their boards. Brill.

I saw others, the boy learners,
uncertain foot-pushers, young lads
who kept to the concrete levels,
kitted out in brand-new knee pads
and elbow guards, helmets and gloves,
birthday presents from grans, mums and dads.

The skater boys didn't notice us
as we stood watching their skilled show,
an invisible man and his dog.
The whole scene was cool speed and flow,
the skateboards rattling on concrete.
The dog whined. It was time to go.

Wes Magee
UK

BOXING

Boxing Poem (extract)

Float like a butterfly,
Sting like a bee,
Your hands can't hit
What your eyes can't see.

Muhammad Ali and Drew Bundini Brown
USA

JUDO

On the Outside a Judoka...

On the outside a Judoka
Is calm and beautiful
Like a clean willow tree
But on the inside
A red flame is burning
This is the way, this is the Life
Like the eternal snows on Mount Fuji
Never ending
Revere Judo, Love Judo, Our Judo

Anonymous
Japan. Translated from Japanese by Philip S. Porter
USA

34

My Puppy Punched Me in the Eye

My puppy punched me in the eye.
   My rabbit whacked my ear.
My ferret gave a frightful cry
   and roundhouse kicked my rear.

My lizard flipped me upside down.
   My kitten kicked my head.
My hamster slammed me to the ground
   and left me nearly dead.

So my advice? Avoid regrets;
   no matter what you do,
don't ever let your family pets
   take lessons in kung fu.

Kenn Nesbitt
USA

Tennis Doubles Trouble

My doubles partner's really bad.
We never win. It makes me mad.
I'd trade him but he'd get so sad.
I really wish I never had
Teamed for doubles with my dad.

Greg Pincus
USA

Let's Play Ping-Pong!

Sing a song
    Of ping-pong
        Come along –
            Let's play!

                Rat-a-tat
            Bounce and pat
        Ball and bat –
Let's play!

Fast and fun
    Hit and run
        Till it's done –
            Let's play!

            To succeed
        You will need
    Spin and speed –
Let's play!

Debjani Chatterjee & Brian D'Arcy
India & UK and Eire & UK

Netball

When
trying
to score
at netball
it helps
if you're
more
than
usually
normally
excess-
ively
extra-
ordinar-
ily
tall.

Ann Bonner
UK

BASEBALL

Take Me Out to the Ball Game

Take me out to the ball game,
Take me out with the crowd.
Buy me some peanuts and cracker jack,
I don't care if I never get back,
Let me root, root, root for the home team,
If they don't win it's a shame.
For it's one, two, three strikes, you're out,
At the old ball game.

Jack Norworth
USA

Baseball

Baseball the game of my life
I play it every day and night
Hit the ball over the wall
Run the bases, win it all.

Ryan Banks
USA

40

Basketball

When the ball slams hard and heavy
into my hand, and I lift it off
for that layup,
the world shrinks into
one small circle,
and time stops
while I hang in the air.
The net holds nothing but stars
till the ball swishes through
and applause surges in
from the galaxies.
The net fills again with stars.
The whole gym seems full of light.
I feel as if I am shining.

Grace Butcher
USA

Kite Flying

Soaring upwards to play among rain-clouds,
Laughing with the elements, child of the wind;
Clowning, uncaring, pioneering spirit,
Shaking your proud head, fluttering a shiny tail,
Fashioned of craft and simple cunning.
Riding the currents of airborne ecstasy,
You surf freedom's waves, sniff Monsoon magic.
Rebel, straining at the string of love and pain,
Do you acknowledge the fist that holds you tight,
The clutch of a child who is tied to the earth?
Do you feel the large bright eyes that follow you,
The heart uplifted with you, racing, daring,
Cart-wheeling and tumbling in the breeze;
Wild Pegasus, galloping, fun-frolicking,
Leaping and somersaulting among rain-clouds,
Laughing with the elements, child of the wind?

Debjani Chatterjee
India & UK

RIDING

My Pony

I took my pony to the show;
he didn't really want to go,
but looked so cute with plaited mane
although perhaps a little vain.
He stamped his hoof and shook his head
and tried to get back to his bed.
But when at last we reached the show,
I think he really seemed to know
that if we tried hard in our test,
we could do well – perhaps be best.
So, in we went to walk and trot
and he enjoyed it quite a lot.
One final canter for the crowd
who clapped for him and cheered out loud.
The judges too seemed pleased to see
how well-behaved we both could be,
and I still can't believe it yet –
we won our first 1st prize rosette!

Brian D'Arcy
UK & Eire

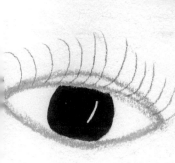

Right Royal (extract)

He moved in his box with a restless tread,
His eyes like sparks in his lovely head,
Ready to run between the roar
Of the stands that face the Straight once more;
Ready to race, though blown, though beat,
As long as his will could lift his feet;
Ready to burst his heart to pass
Each gasping horse in that street of grass.

John Masefield
UK

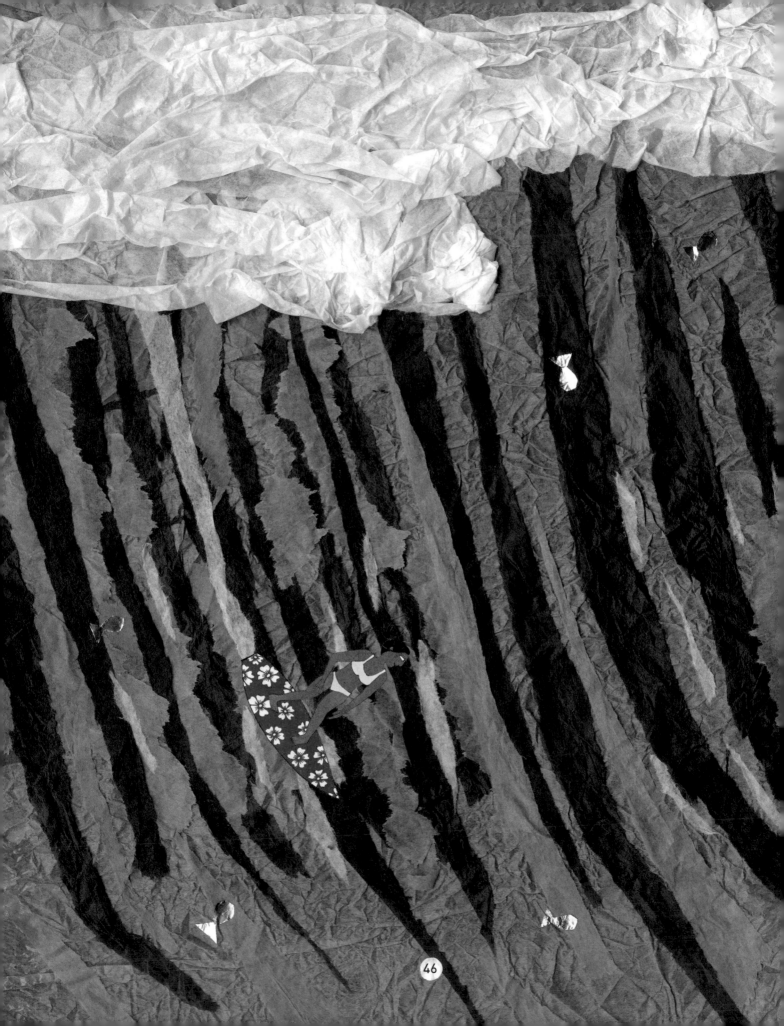

Surfing

It's not the waves you catch,
How hard or how strong.
It's the wind in your hair,
The ocean's song.
Knowing you can't,
Almost certain you can.
Endless blue,
With a bare sight of land.
Getting to know the oceans,
Dolphins and fish your friends.
Too many mistakes,
That you need now not mend.
The loss of all worries,
The bad, the worst.
Nothing is practised,
Nothing rehearsed.
The surfer's only knowledge
Of what's going on,
Is the coming of the waves,
In the wake of the dawn.

Sasha Walker/Mills
USA

47

FOOTBALL

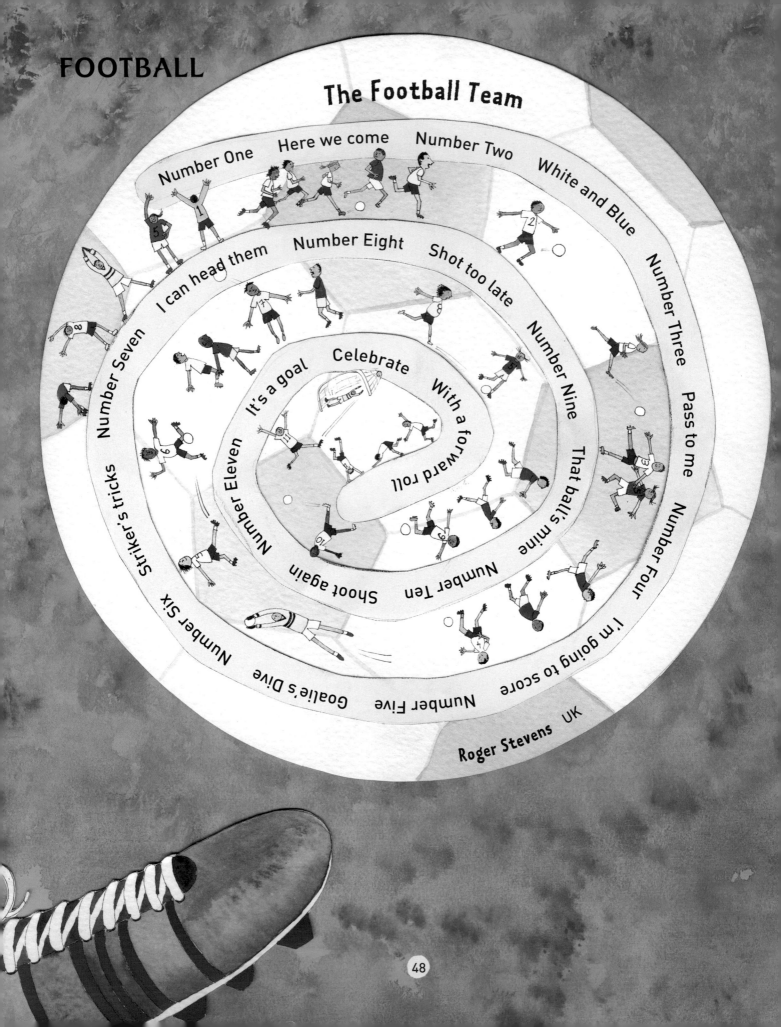

The Football Team

Number One Here we come Number Two White and Blue Number Three Pass to me Number Four I'm going to score Number Five Goalie's Dive Number Six Striker's tricks Number Seven I can head them Number Eight Shot too late Number Nine That ball's mine Number Ten Shoot again Number Eleven It's a goal Celebrate With a forward roll

Roger Stevens UK

Alumnus Football (extract)

For when the One Great Scorer comes
To mark against your name,
He writes – not that you won or lost –
But how you played the game.

Grantland Rice
USA

49

About the Sports and Games

American Football has overtaken baseball as America's most popular spectator sport. It is played between two sides, each with 11 players on the field.. There are up to 7 refereeing officials in control of the game. The game alternates between periods of little, or no, action (where the attackers plan their next attack and the defenders try to anticipate the attack) and periods of fast physical attack and defence action.

Baseball A 1744 children's book *A Little Pretty Pocketbook* by British publisher John Newbery includes a rhyme entitled 'Base-Ball'. This is the first known reference to baseball in print, but it actually meant the game rounders, an ancestor of modern baseball. Jack Norworth's song *'Take Me Out to the Ball Game'* is considered baseball's anthem.

Basketball is one of the world's most popular and widely watched team sports. It is played on a marked rectangular court with a basket at each end that is 18 inches in diameter and exactly 10 feet above the ground. Points are scored by shooting the ball into the basket. For men the official ball is 9.4inches diameter and for women 9.1inches diameter. Five players from each of two competing teams are on the court at one time and substitutions are unlimited but can only be made when play is stopped.

Boxing evolved from 16th and 18th century prize-fights in Great Britain. In 1867 rules were drafted by John Chambers for amateur championships to be held at Lillie Bridge in London. The rules were published under the patronage of the Marquess of Queensberry and are still internationally known as the Marquess of Queensberry Rules.

Chess is a complex board game for two players, involving strategy and tactics, the object being to checkmate (capture) your opponent's king. Chess Grand Masters (the best players in the world) can work out the advantages and the risks of about three move options per second, and the most powerful chess playing computers can evaluate several million options per second. But when Grand Masters play against computers, the games are still remarkably equal.

Circle Games Many games for children are described as 'circle games' when they involve a group of children being in a circle; circle games have no 'loser', every child 'wins' because they get to play.

Clapping Games (or **hand games**) are played in many different countries, usually by two players. They involve clapping in time to a song or rhyme. Claps follow patterns such as clapping your own hands and then clapping one or both hands of a partner for a set number of times.

Cricket is a popular team game in many countries, for a total of 22 players. Its rules and tradition are strongly associated with a sense of sportsmanship, so much so that the word 'cricket' is often used as a metaphor for fair play. If something is unfair, we say that it is 'just not cricket'!

Computer Games are video games played on a personal computer or smartphone. They have become more and more sophisticated over the last few years and now include: Action-Adventure, Role–playing, Simulation and Strategy.

Cycling competitions were organised in many parts of the world quite soon after the invention of the bicycle. Races became popular in the 1890s, with events across Europe, the USA and Japan. The most famous bicycle race is the annual Tour de France, which was first held in 1903. The modern Tour de France consists of 21 day-long segments (stages) over a 23-day period involving time trials, steep climbs in the Pyrenees and the Alps, and the celebratory finish on the Champs-Élysées in Paris.

Diving competitions generally consist of three disciplines: 1 metre and 3 metre springboards, and the platform, which in major diving events is from a 10 metre height. Divers perform a set number of dives involving somersaults and twists and are judged on how well they complete all aspects of the dive. Each judge gives a score out of ten which is multiplied by a difficulty factor allocated to the dive. The diver with the highest final score wins.

Football (Association Football), also known as soccer, is played by over 250 million people in over 200 countries, making it the world's most popular sport. The Laws of the Game were originally set up in England by the Football Association in 1863 and have evolved since then. Association Football is governed internationally by FIFA—Fédération Internationale de Football Association, which organises the FIFA World Cup every four years. Women have been playing Association Football since the first recorded women's game in 1895 in North London. The FIFA Women's World Cup was inaugurated in 1991 and is held every four years.

Ice Hockey is a fast-paced sport, played between two teams skating on ice, each with six players. A team usually has four sets of three attackers, three pairs of defenders and two goalkeepers. Each team tries to score goals by hitting the 'puck' into the opponents' net.. Ice hockey is most popular in North America and Europe. The first organized game was played in Canada on March 3, 1875.

Judo means 'gentle way'; it is a modern martial art, combat and Olympic sport created in Japan in 1882 by Jigoro Kano. Its object is to throw or take down an opponent to the ground, or to immobilize or subdue an opponent with a grappling movement, or force an opponent to submit. Strikes and thrusts by hands, feet and weapons are not allowed in judo competitions.

Kiting or Kite Flying began in China and India nearly 3000 years ago and is a popular sport in many countries. Marco Polo brought back stories of kites to Europe in the late 13th century, and 16th and 17th century European sailors brought back kites as souvenirs from Asia. In the Indian sub-continent and in Afghanistan kite fighting, in which players try to snag or cut other kites' strings, is hugely popular. Weifang in China has the world's largest kite museum and hosts an important kite festival.

Kung Fu and **Wushu** refer to Chinese martial arts. Wushu literally means 'martial art'. It is formed from the two words 'wu', meaning 'martial' or 'military' and 'shu' which means 'discipline', 'skill' or 'method'. 'Wushu' is a more precise term for the modern exhibition and full-contact sport involving bare-hands and weapons. It was only in the late twentieth century that the term Kung Fu began to be used in relation to martial arts.

Netball was first played in England in the 1890s, and was derived from Basketball, which had been earlier invented in America. In 1985 it was included for the first time at the World Games, a sporting competition held every four years for sports not played at the Olympic Games. Today netball is most popular in Britain and the Commonwealth countries, particularly in schools and universities.

Pole Vaulting originated in Europe, where the pole was used to cross water-filled canals; this type of vaulting aimed at distance rather than height. In modern pole vaulting it is height that counts. Today's carbon fibre poles are much lighter than the wood, bamboo or metal vaulting poles of the past, so competitors can vault much higher.

Racing (Horse Racing) is a sport in which specially bred racehorses race against each other, ridden by 'jockeys', on a circular grass track or 'racecourse'. Sometimes the race is over fences (steeplechase).

Riding (Horse Riding) The best estimate of when horses were first ridden is 4500 BC. Since that time the horse has played an important role both in war and in peaceful pursuits such as transportation, trade and agriculture and a wide variety of competitive sports and pastimes. Equestrianism (show-jumping, dressage and eventing) was first included in the Olympic Games at Stockholm in 1912.

Running competitions were first held at religious festivals in Greece, Egypt, Asia and Africa's Rift Valley. The origins of Olympic and Marathon running can be found in Greek myth and legend, and the first recorded Olympic Games took place in Olympia in Greece in 776 BC.

Scrabble is the world's most popular word game for children and adults, and is played in many languages, both as a board game and as a computer game. It lasts for about an hour and relies on a broad vocabulary as well as strategy. International tournaments are held.

Shot Put is a track and field event which involves putting (throwing in a pushing motion) a heavy metal ball – the *shot* – as far as possible. The first ever shot put events took place in the Middle Ages, when soldiers held competitions in which they hurled cannonballs. In the 16th century King Henry VIII of England was noted for his prowess in court competitions of weight and hammer throwing.

Skateboarding is an action sport that involves riding and performing jumps and tricks, using a board on wheels – a skateboard. Since the 1970s skate parks have been constructed specifically for use by skateboarders, bikers and inline skaters.

Snakes and Ladders is a worldwide classic board game, invented as Moksha Patam (or 'Winning Salvation') in ancient India. The snakes on the board represent vices that pull you down while the ladders are virtues that help you to rise. The board has a hundred numbered squares and players throw a dice to see how many squares they can move. The first to reach square 100, the goal of *moksha* or salvation, wins. The game was introduced to England in 1892, and in 1943 Milton Bradley introduced it in the USA as Chutes and Ladders. The modern Indian version is Shaap-Ludo or Saap-Ludo.

Surfing is a water sport in which the participant rides a surfboard on a breaking wave. There are three major subdivisions within stand-up surfing known as long-boarding, short-boarding, and stand-up paddle surfing. The Guinness Book of World Records recognises a 78 metre wave-ride which was filmed as the largest wave ever surfed.

Swimming is one of the most popular recreational activities, and you can do it on your own, or race against other people. In some countries swimming lessons are a compulsory part of the school curriculum. There are four main strokes: front crawl, breaststroke, backstroke and butterfly.

Swinging – A swing is a hanging seat, usually for children, who sit on the swing and kick off from the ground. Young children are helped to swing by someone pushing gently, while older children swing themselves. At the highest points on a swing the swinger is weightless!

Table Tennis or Ping-Pong originated in Britain during the 1880s. The game may have been first developed by British military officers in India or South Africa. By 1901 table tennis tournaments were being organized and an unofficial world championship was held in 1902. During the early 1900s, the game was banned in Russia because the rulers at the time believed that playing the game had a bad effect on players' eyesight!

Tennis is played between two players (singles) or between two teams of two players (doubles). It involves hitting a tennis ball over a net, trying to hit it so that the opponent can't hit it back. The modern game of tennis originated in Birmingham, England, in the late 19th century and has close connections to the older racquet sport of *real tennis*. The rules of tennis have not changed much since the 1890s, but a recent addition to professional tennis has been the adoption of electronic review technology, so there can be no argument about whether the ball is in or out!

Tobogganing is a traditional form of snow transport used by the Innu and Cree people of northern Canada. In modern times it is used for fun, to carry one or more people down a snow-covered hill, and is also known as sledging. The winter sport of bobsleigh is a high-speed racing version in which teams of two or four make timed runs down specially built, icy, twisting tracks.